Getting Started

When it's time to open up the world of mathematics for young learners, it can happen anytime, anywhere. There is a veritable treasure of mathematics inspiration to be found in the nursery rhymes you learn every year.

How Many Rhymes Do We Know?

Ask children to take turns reciting nursery rhymes they already know. List the rhymes on the chalkboard or a chart. When you have finished the list, have children count the titles.

> Rock-a-bye baby
> Little Bo-peep
> Hickory, dickory, dock
> Mary, Mary, quite contrary
> Rain, rain, go away
> Baa, Baa, Black Sheep
> Hey, diddle, diddle
> Old King Cole
> Pease Porridge

My Own Nursery Rhyme Book

Each of the rhymes in this book is written on an individual page with a simple illustration. Reproduce these pages for each child as you go along. Have them color the pictures, then save the pages until you have completed all of the rhymes. They may put their pages together into a construction paper folder to take home and share with their families.

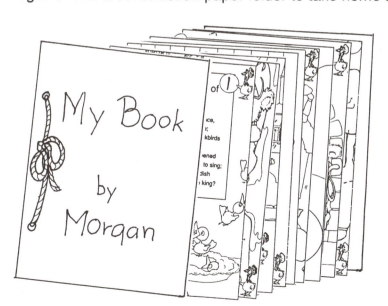

Each page has a Mother Goose and a circle on it. Have children number the pages by placing each number in the circle.

Sing a Song of Sixpence

Sing a song of sixpence,
    a pocketful of rye;
Four-and-twenty blackbirds
    baked in a pie.
When the pie was opened
    the birds began to sing;
Wasn't that a dainty dish
    to set before the king?

Math with Nursery Rhymes

"Four-and-Twenty"

Materials:
• 24 or more backbird patterns (See page 4.)
• crayons

Directions:
Give the children copies of the bird patterns. Allow them to color the birds. Encourage students to create fanciful birds; they need not be all black.

Collect the finished birds and set them out on a low table where they are visible to everyone. First ask the children to help you count out 4 blackbirds and set these aside in a corner of the table. Now to the larger task at hand. Ask the children to recite with you as you count out 20 birds. They may need help through the teens. Set these 20 aside, and remove any extras from the table for now. Announce that you now have "four-and-twenty" birds.

Ask if anyone knows another way of saying the number "four-and-twenty." Explain that "four-and-twenty" is simply an old-fashioned way of saying 24. To illustrate, count the birds again, from 1 to 24.

Extension:
Practice the place value of larger numbers by making many blackbirds and following the procedure described above.

Note: Use these birds with the activities on pages 3 and 6.

Sing a Song of Sixpence
Blackbird Patterns

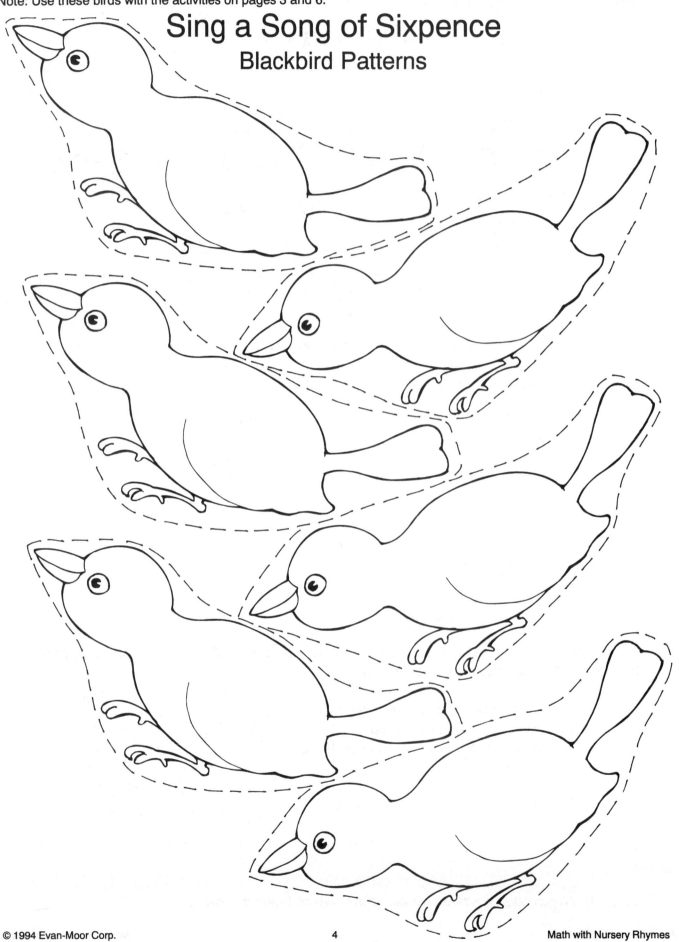

Math with Nursery Rhymes

Bird Watch

1. Go for a "bird watching" walk. Keep a tally of the number of birds seen on the walk.

2. Share books about the care and feeding of pet birds.

3. Share pictures of wild birds. Discuss their sizes and shapes. Point out the number of claws/toes on their feet.

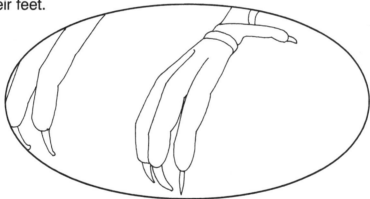

4. Have children bring in pictures of birds from newspapers and magazines to share with the class. Use these to make a bird counting book.

   a. Child pastes bird pictures to a sheet of colored construction paper, counts the number of birds and writes the number of birds on the page.

   b. Put all the pages together in a cover.

5. Take a trip to the local pet store or zoo to see different types of birds.

   a. Count the different birds found in each cage as you view the birds.
   b. Which cage holds the most birds? Which holds the least?

The Royal Pie

Materials:
- colored blackbird patterns (See page 4.)
- jumbo cotton balls
- glitter
- a large piece of colored poster board
- glue

Directions:
Cut a very large circle from the posterboard for the pie plate.

Children can help make the "stuffing" for the pie. Pour the jumbo cotton balls into a bowl, and let each child count out 6 (or any other appropriate number) and return to the work area. Children should pull the cotton balls apart so that they are fluffy. While they are doing this, coat the posterboard circle with glue. Then have children come up, two by two, to press their cotton ball pie filling onto the posterboard pie "plate."

When the pie is full of fluffy filling (you may even want to add on a second layer), let the children dip the corners of their birds into the glue and then press them gently onto the pie. For a finishing effect, pour the glitter into a bowl, and let each child sprinkle a pinch full of glitter onto the pie.

Finally, count the number of blackbirds in your royal pie. Point out that the number of blackbirds in the pie should be equal to the number of children in the room, since each child put one bird in the pie.

How Many Blackbirds in the Pie?

Reproduce the pie and bird pattern on page 8. Cut the pie out of white felt. Cut a set of 24 birds out of black and orange felt. Use the pattern to practice...

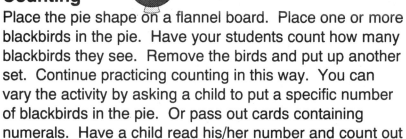

Counting

Place the pie shape on a flannel board. Place one or more blackbirds in the pie. Have your students count how many blackbirds they see. Remove the birds and put up another set. Continue practicing counting in this way. You can vary the activity by asking a child to put a specific number of blackbirds in the pie. Or pass out cards containing numerals. Have a child read his/her number and count out that many blackbirds onto the pie shape.

Computation

Place a set of birds on the pie. Ask children to tell you how many birds they see, then ask how many more you need in order to have (give a number).

Place a set of birds on the pie. Ask children to tell you how many birds they see, then ask how many will be left if (give a number) fly away.

Center Activity

Make a set of pies from construction paper. Hinge two together at the top. Write a numeral on the "crust " of the pie and glue a corresponding set of blackbirds "inside" the pie. Make a set of blackbirds. Cut these out and store in an envelope or resealable baggie. Display the pies and blackbirds in a center or attach them to a low bulletin board.

Children read the number and count out that many birds. They lift the top of the pie to check their answers.

You can make a variation of this center activity for children ready to practice computation. Write a problem on the top of the pie and the answer inside. Children use the black-birds to solve the problems, then look inside to check their answers.

Note: Reproduce this pattern to use with the activities on page 7.

8

Math with Nursery Rhymes

Lucy Locket

Lucy Locket lost her pocket,
Kitty Fisher found it;
There was not a penny in it,
But a ribbon round it!

Math with Nursery Rhymes

Money in My Pocket

Explain to students that the pocket in this rhyme is a small purse.
Discuss other types of pockets and pocketbooks they are familiar with.

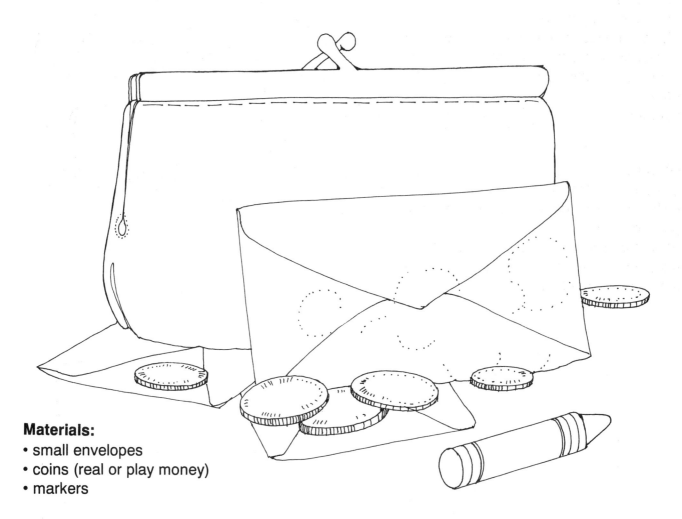

Materials:
• small envelopes
• coins (real or play money)
• markers

Directions:
Mark each envelope with a single number from 1 to 10. Set these out on a table along with a pile of coins. Allow each child a chance to go to the table and fill the envelopes with the correct number of coins.

Assessment Tip:
Make a set of ten numbered envelopes for each child and label with their names. Each day repeat this activity with different materials: buttons, large sequins, dry cereal O's, etc. When *you* empty the envelopes each day, you can see how they're doing.

Extension:
If your students are ready to work with larger coins, write money amounts on envelopes. Have children read the amount and put the correct number of coins in the envelopes.

A Penny Pocketbook

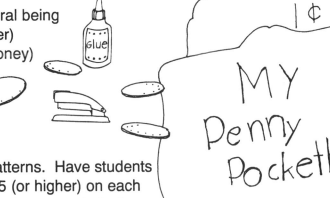

Materials:
- pocketbook pattern
  (one copy for each numeral being
  included plus a front cover)
- coins (reproduce play money)
- glue
- stapler

Directions:
Cut out the pocketbook patterns. Have students write a numeral from 1 to 5 (or higher) on each pattern piece. They are to glue one coin to the page marked 1, 2 coins on 2, etc. Have children put their pages in numerical order and staple them together.

What's in Lucy Locket's Pocket?

Bring in a large pocketbook. Put various numbers of items in the pocketbook (one type at a time). Have a child come up and empty the pocketbook, count the items, and give the total. Have a second child write the numeral on the chalkboard.

Ask children what number we use for "less than one" or "nothing" (zero). Give funny examples and have children name the amount.

"How many pink giraffes are in Lucy's pocket?"
"How many school buses are in Lucy's pocket?"

Have children come up with examples of their own.

Pass out sheets of drawing paper. Have children fold the paper in half, then in half again to make four boxes. (Discuss the idea of half and fourth as you do this.) Have children draw a pocket in each box, then draw something funny or exciting in each of the pockets. Finally, they write the number of items in each pocket in the same box. See if any clever child has a "zero" pocket!

It is always fun to act out a rhyme. Have children recite the first three lines of the rhyme and act it out. You add something new each time they come to the last line - and they act that out too!

Lucy Locket lost her pocket
(shrug and look around)
Kitty Fisher found it *(stoop down to pick it up)*
There was not a penny in it
(open hands and look inside)

But...an elephant in it!
(children act out the animal)

But...a trumpet *(or other instrument)* in it!
(children pretend to blow the horn)

But...a bell *(or other object)* in it!
(children pretend to ring the bell)

   Math with Nursery Rhymes

Handy Spandy,
Jack-a-dandy

Handy Spandy, Jack-a-dandy,

Loves plum cake and sugar candy.

He bought some at the grocer's shop,

And out he came, hop, hop, hop.

   Math with Nursery Rhymes

Who Likes Candy?

What Kind of Candy do You Like?

Ask children to tell you their favorite kinds of candy. Make a list of their answers. Point to each candy type and ask children to raise their hand if they like that kind. Select a child who does not have his/her hand up to count the response each time. Write down the number by the candy name. When the class has voted on each candy type, have them read the numbers and decide which candy the most children liked and which candy the fewest children liked.

My Favorite Candy

Make a simple bar graph on butcher paper. Place pictures of the candy shown above along the bottom of the paper. Pass out squares of colored paper. Have children vote on their favorite candy on the list by placing their squares of paper above the candy name. Talk about the results.

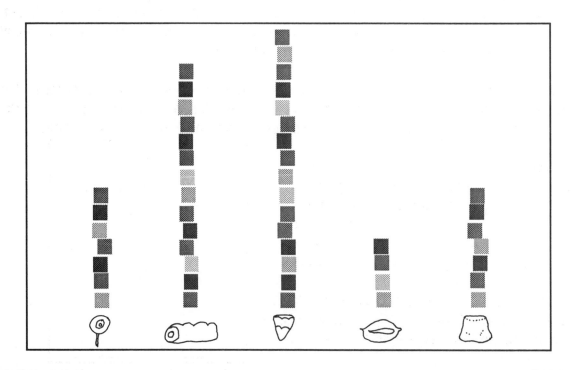

14

Rock Candy Crystals

Explain that most candy has sugar in it. In fact, you can make a kind of candy with just sugar and water. (You may want to talk about crystals and how they form at this time.)

Select children to help with the measurement of ingredients. Discuss how the various measuring instruments are used. (After doing this activity you may want to set up a measuring center. Make measuring cups and spoons of different types available. Display containers of varying shapes and ask children to determine which containers hold the same amount.)

Materials:
- 1 cup (236 ml) granulated sugar
- 1/2 cup (118 ml) water
- clear glass jar
- cotton string
- small, clean nut or paper clip for a weight
- tape
- record form (page 16)

- measuring cup
- small saucepan
- wooden spoon
- pencil
- food coloring (optional)
- calendar
- hot plate or electric skillet

Directions:
Mark off an area around the table where you have your heat source as a "stop" sign for children. Be sure they can see, but are still far enough away to be safe from heat or splattering sugar water.

Make sure all utensils are clean. Select children to measure and place the water and sugar in a small saucepan. Select a child to stir the sugar water until the sugar begins to dissolve. Have all children move outside the marked barrier. Now heat the water and sugar on low, stirring constantly. Continue heating until the sugar is completely dissolved. Boil one minute, but don't burn. Drop in a few drops of food coloring if desired. You might want to mix several colors of solution for a colorful observation activity. Pour the syrup into the jars.

Tie weights to the ends of the strings. Secure the free ends between two pieces of tape. Drop the weight and string into the jar and secure with more tape. Put the jar aside in a safe place to stand. Carefully remove any crystals that form at the surface so that the water can evaporate.

Make an observation chart using a calendar with large squares for drawings or comments for each day of the week. In the beginning, nothing much will happen. Children might simply make a check, noting that they have observed the solution. Later, around halfway through the second week, crystals will begin to form. Children can draw what they see on their individual observation logs. When the sugar crystals are complete, divide them up so each child can have a sample of the tasty result!

Sugar Candy Crystals
Observation Log

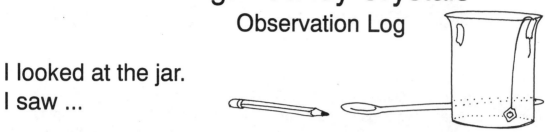

I looked at the jar.
I saw ...

Monday	**Tuesday**	**Wednesday**	**Thursday**	**Friday**
Monday	**Tuesday**	**Wednesday**	**Thursday**	**Friday**

Math with Nursery Rhymes

Fill the Candy Jar

Materials:
• a see-through jar
• real pieces of wrapped candy
  or candy shapes cut from
  construction paper
• set of number word cards

Directions:
Review the number word cards to be sure your students can read them. Have a child select
a card, read it aloud, then put that many pieces of candy into the candy jar. You can reverse
the process by putting candy in the jar, having a child come up and count the candy, then find
the correct number word card.

Extension:
The same pieces can be used to practice adding and subtracting by substituting equation cards
for the number word cards.

Make a large candy jar on the floor using masking tape. Tell your children they are going to be
the "candy" that will go into the jar. Select a group of children to be the first set of candy. Give
each child a large candy shape cut from colored construction paper. Have them stand near the
jar as you tell a number "story." They move in and out of the jar as the story continues. For
example...

"Mr. Martinez had a candy store. One morning he put
two pieces of red candy in the candy jar. Then he put
three pieces of green candy in the jar. How many pieces
are in the jar now?"

"Soon a little girl came into the store and bought one
green candy and one red candy. How much candy
did she buy?"

"Mr. Martinez counted the candy he had left in his jar. He had _____ pieces left."

Handy Spandy Numbers and Movement

Stand in a circle with the children and recite the first three lines of the verse, alternately slapping knees and clapping hands. Have children take turns saying a line going around the circle. When you get to "And out he came," the child saying that line jumps to the center. Then you call out a movement to the verse. It doesn't matter if the word does not rhyme. You are practicing listening, movement, and counting at this point. The child in the center acts it out. That child then returns to the circle, and the activity continues. Example:

Handy Spandy, Jack-a-dandy,
Loves plum cake and sugar candy.
He bought some at the grocer's shop,

...and out he came with three hops!
(Child hops three times.)

...and out he came with five claps!
(Child claps five times.)

...and out he came with two spins!
(Child spins two times.)

...and out he came with four stomps!
(Child stomps four times.)

..and out he came with one bow!
(Child bows once.)

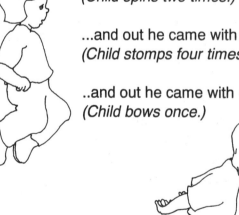

Extension:
Play Candyland ™, being sure to have players count out the number of steps it takes them to reach the next color marked on the board.

                                       Math with Nursery Rhymes

Math Skills: money; counting

Set up a play "snack store" in class. You don't need to sell "plum cake" and "sugar candy" to make this a useful teaching tool. Use the store as a snack time center.

Determine the times the "store" will be open. Demonstrate how children will move through the center before you introduce the activity to the class. You may want to make some sort of routing chart to post by the center.

1. Set up a table in front of a bulletin board containing the name of the "store."

2. Make up price cards to display with the snacks that are "for sale." Provide a selection of healthy treats such as raisins, pretzels, nuts, vegetable or fruit bits, etc. Encourage parents to help provide the items for the center. Your cafeteria or a local grocery store may be willing to help also.

3. Provide students with play money to use to "purchase" their snacks. You may want to extend the activity by having children "earn" the money by doing special activities around the classroom (watering plants, cleaning chalkboard, putting toys and books away, etc.).

4. Select someone to be the storekeeper and someone to "bag" the snacks.

Variations:
Place toys, games or books in the center. Have someone new each day be the store-keeper. Children "buy" a toy, game or book to use for the length of the center time. The items are then returned to the center to be used again the next day.

Hickory,
Dickory,
Dock

Hickory, Dickory, Dock,

The mouse ran up the clock,

The clock struck one,

The mouse ran down,

Hickory, Dickory, Dock!

Math with Nursery Rhymes

The Clock Shop

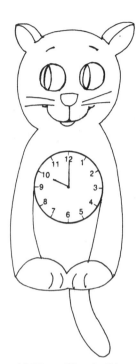

You will be doing two activities with this form, recognizing geometric shapes and telling time to the hour.

Talk about what a clock looks like. Have children describe the classroom clock in terms of its parts and it geometric shape. Bring in real clocks in different shapes or find photographs in magazines or catalogs to use. Have children determine the shape of each clock. Most clocks will be circles, squares, or rectangles. Place colored shapes up on a wall to refer to as a model for the children.

What Shape Is It?

Ask children what shapes clocks usually come in. Give children copies of The Clock Shop form on page 22. Discuss the different shapes of the clocks on their sheets, asking them to name and describe a triangle, a circle, a rectangle, and a square.

Have the children color in all the clocks following your oral directions.

> *Color in all the triangular clocks red.*
> *Color all the rectangular clocks blue.*
> *Color all the square clocks green.*
> *Color all of the clocks that are a circle purple.*

Assessment Tip:

Walk around the room while the children are coloring. Carry four small objects in the palm of your hand: a triangle, a square, a rectangle and a circle. Hold out your hand and ask a child to point to the object that is the shape you name.

What Time Is It?

Have children look at the hands on the clock. Explain that the short hand tells us what hour it is. Have them look at each clock face and tell you the hour.

Have children look at the digital clock faces. Explain that the numbers in front of the dots tell us what hour it is. Have them look at each digital clock and tell you the hour.

Have them draw lines between clocks to match those telling the same hour.

The Clock Shop

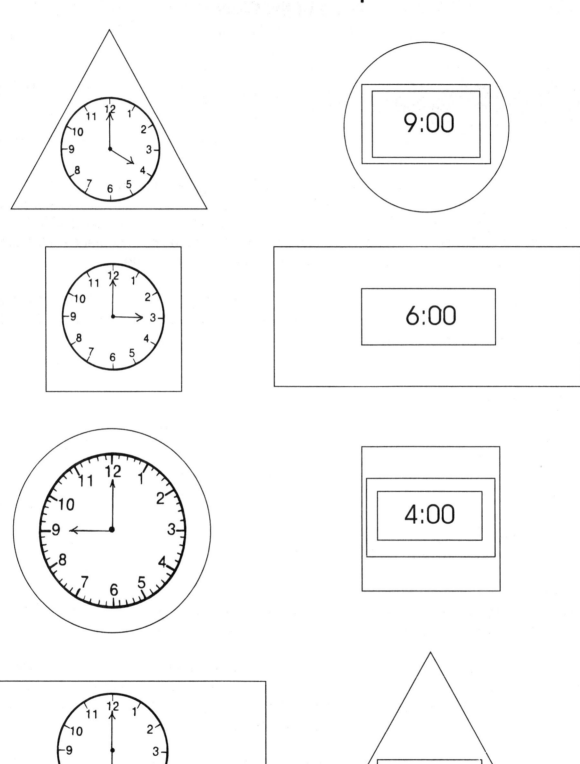

Math with Nursery Rhymes

Tick-Tock Goes My Clock

Parts of the Clock

A Flannel Board Activity

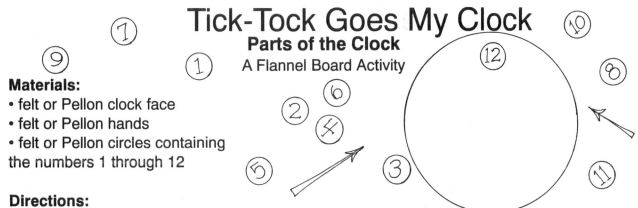

Materials:
- felt or Pellon clock face
- felt or Pellon hands
- felt or Pellon circles containing the numbers 1 through 12

Directions:

Place the clock face on the flannel board. Pass out the numbered circles. Have children look at the classroom clock to see where the numbers go. Have the child with 12 come up and place his/her number in the correct place on the clock face. Have the child with 6 come up and place it on the clock. Continue until all numbers are in the correct place on the clock face. Have children read the numbers around the clock starting at one.

Place the hour and minute hands on the clock. Have the minute hand on 12. Move the hour hand to different positions to practice telling time to the hour. Then have children place the hour hand to show the time you say.

My Own Clock

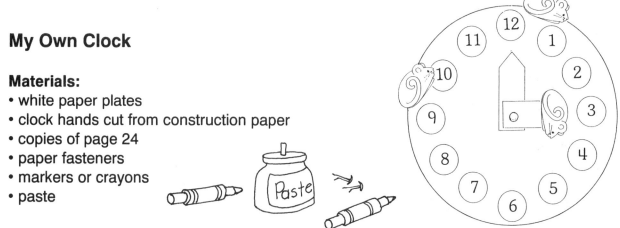

Materials:
- white paper plates
- clock hands cut from construction paper
- copies of page 24
- paper fasteners
- markers or crayons
- paste

Directions:

Give each child a paper plate , a copy of the hands and number form, and a paper fastener. Have children color and cut out the numbers and the little mice.

Have them look at a real clock as a model of where the numbers go on their clocks. Have them place the numbers around the clock in the correct place. After you have checked number placement, they can paste the numbers down. Have them paste one mouse to the end of the hour hand so the mouse can "run around" their clocks.

Show children how to attach the hands with the paper fastener. Have them work together to put the hands on their own clocks. If your class needs more help with this step, call on volunteers or cross-grade tutors.

As a group activity, you can practice moving the hands around the clocks to show 1 o'clock, 2 o'clock, and so on. Do "half-hours" when your children are ready.

Note: Reproduce this page to use with the activity on page 23.

Math with Nursery Rhymes

Why Do I Need to Tell Time?

Have children think of all the places out in the world that they might find clocks: e.g., the airport, bus or train station; school; outside on building clock towers. Ask your students to explain why it is important to be able to tell time. List all the reasons they come up with. Guide them by your questions to add to the list. After you have discussed how they use time in their lives, create class or individual books about important times during the day.

Materials:
•several copies of the form below
•crayons or markers

Directions:
Give each child or group of children several copies of the form. Ask them to draw something important they do during the day that is connected with a certain time. Help them draw hands on their clocks to show the time the events take place, then write a word, phrase, or sentence about what is happening. If you make class books put all the pages together inside a cover saying "Our Day." If children do individual books, have them put the pages in time order and make covers.

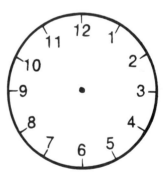

Diddle, Diddle, Dumpling, My Son John

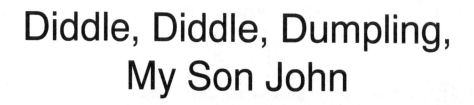

Diddle, diddle, dumpling, my son John,

Went to bed with his stockings on;

One shoe off, and one shoe on,

Diddle, diddle, dumpling, my son John.

Math with Nursery Rhymes

Right Shoe Off, Left Shoe On

Materials:
• an extra large slipper that will be easy for all children to slip on
• stickers

Directions:
Children should take off their shoes and sit in stocking feet in a circle. Each child places a sticker on the toe of his/her right sock. Begin the game by having the person with the slipper pass it to the child on her/his right. Chant this variation of the rhyme together:

Group:	Diddle, diddle dumpling, my friend *(child's name)* *(everyone shouts child's name)* Went to sleep with his stockings on *(fold hands under chin as if sleeping)*
Teacher:	Right shoe on (or left), left shoe off *(or right)* *(child puts slipper on the correct foot called for)*
Group:	Diddle, diddle dumpling, my friend *(child's name)* *(everyone shouts child's name)*

That child then passes the slipper to the right, and the game begins again until everyone has had a turn or time is up.

Assessment Tip:
After everyone has had a chance to play the circle game, do a simple Simon Says game, focusing on very basic skills using the terms left and right.

"Tap your right knee."
"Pull your right ear."
"Cover your left eye," etc.

Note who seems to have the left/right concept and who does not.

Note: Reproduce this page for each child. Explain that all of the creatures on the page want to sleep with their stockings on too. Have children draw a socking on each foot and then write the number in the square to tell how many stockings each creature needs to stay warm at night.

Going to Bed With My Stockings On!
How many stockings do I need?

Match the Socks

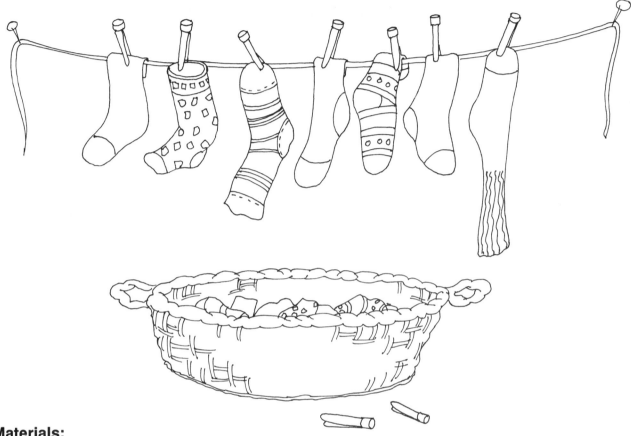

Materials:
- yarn or heavy string
- clothespins
- several pairs of socks

Directions:
Place a "clothesline" on a bulletin board low enough for children to reach. Bring in an interesting collection of socks in different sizes, patterns, etc. Hang up one sock from each pair on the clothesline. Place the others in a "laundry basket." Have children work independently or in pairs to match the socks in the basket with the socks on the line.

When students are finished, have them count:
- how many pairs they have
- how many individual socks they have

Extension:
Some students may be ready to learn how to count by twos using the pairs of socks.

Note: Have your students make each pair a different color.

Match the Pairs

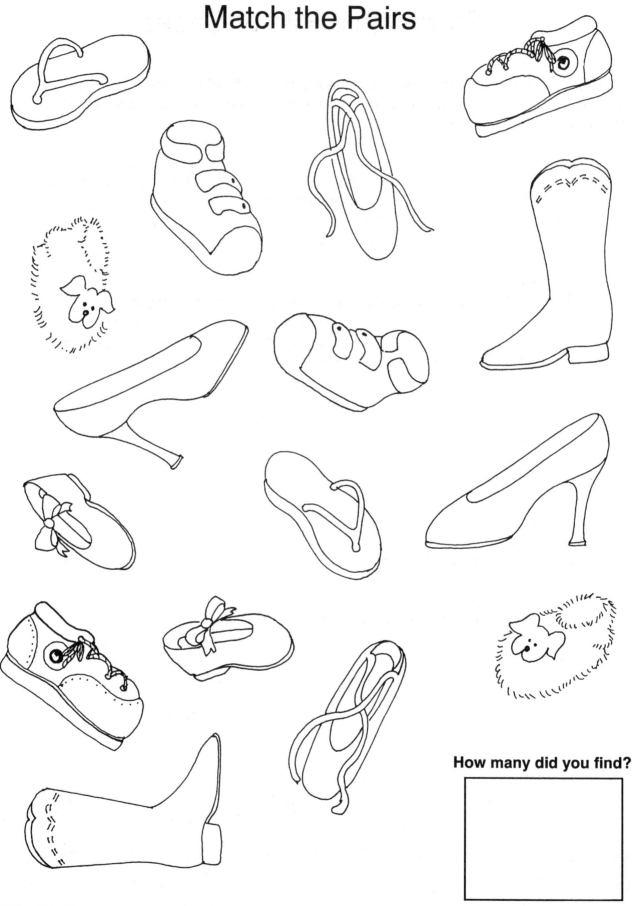

How many did you find?

30

Math with Nursery Rhymes

Start with a Pile of Shoes

Have everyone take off one shoe and place it in the middle of the floor in a pile with all the others. Talk about all the ways you might be able to sort out the shoes. Encouraging children to come up with suggestions.

- color
- length
- what it is made of
- how it closes
- special types of shoes

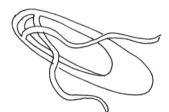

Sorting

Have children find all of the shoes that fit a stated category (brown, lace-up, canvas, etc.) Once the shoes have been sorted, have children count how many fit that categoary. You can extend the activity even further by graphing the results of one or more sorting activities.

Counting

Have children count to answer a specific question.

"How many holes are in the lace-up shoes?"
"How many shoes are in the pile?"
"How many black shoes with buckles do you see?"

Matching

Have children place all shoes of the same type in piles.
After they have sorted the shoes, have them count how many are in each set.

Making Pairs

Have children find their own shoe in the pile to "make a pair."

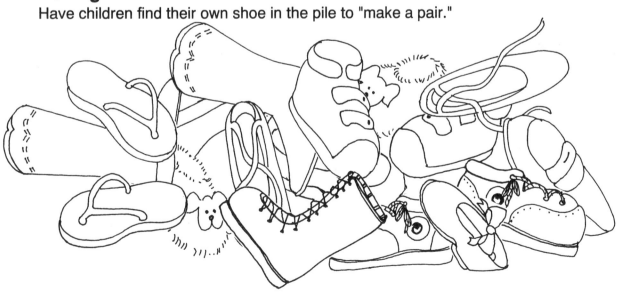

31 Math with Nursery Rhymes

This Little Piggy

The first little piggy went to the market.

The second little piggy stayed home.

The third little piggy had roast beef.

The fourth little piggy had none.

The fifth little piggy went "wee, wee, wee"

All the way home.

Math with Nursery Rhymes

This Little Piggy

One to One Correspondence

Have children work in pairs with bare feet and practice reciting the "little piggies" rhyme. They should tap each other's toes as they recite. Help them learn "first, second, third, fourth, and fifth" before they begin.

Counting by Fives

Practice counting by fives using students own "little piggies." Ask your students to estimate how many toes there are in your class. Write the estimates on the chalkboard. Have children sit bare footed in a circle with feet sticking out into the circle. Go around the circle counting each foot of 5 toes...5, 10, 15, etc. Record the total on the chalkboard. Did anyone make a correct estimate?

Ordinal Numbers

When all socks and shoes are back in place, give each child a sheet of drawing paper. Have them draw a line of five little piggies; then give oral directions to further practice ordinal numbers. "Color the third piggy yellow." "Put purple socks on the first piggy." "Draw a big hat on the fifth piggy." "Make boots on the fourth piggy," etc.

   Math with Nursery Rhymes

Baa, Baa, Black Sheep

Baa, baa, black sheep, have you any wool?

Yes, sir. Yes, sir, three bags full.

One for my master, one for my dame.

And one for the little boy who lives down the lane.

         Math with Nursery Rhymes

Black Sheep's Wool
A Center Activity

Materials:
- black cotton balls
- newspaper
- paper towels or pre-moistened wipes (for wiping fingers)
- five small containers
- record form on page 36

Model the Center Activity:
Place the colored cotton balls on newspaper. Set the "bags" in a row. Now recite the rhyme, substituting a new number of bags of wool each time.

Teacher: Baa, baa, black sheep, have you any wool?
Yes, sir. Yes, sir, (2) bags full.

Children: Baa, baa, black sheep, have you any wool?
Yes, sir. Yes, sir, (2) bags full!

As you recite the number, select a child to come up and fill that many bags. Have children color in their record sheet to show the number of bags you have filled. Now select a child to come up and count the number of cotton balls in the first bag. Have children record that number on the first bag of their record sheet. Do the same with the remaining bags. Finally, have them decide which bag has the most cotton in it and put an X on that bag.

Repeat with other numbers until you are sure your students understand the process.

At the Center:
Set out the bags, cotton balls, and copies of the record form. When children come to the center, they recite their own version of the verse, deciding how many bags to fill each time. Then they fill in the record sheet: color in the bags, count the cotton balls, and cross out the bag containing the most cotton.

Black Cotton Balls

Materials:
- cotton balls
- black powdered tempera paint -1 tbsp (15ml)
- talcum powder - 2 tsp (10ml)
- paper sack

How to prepare:
Color the cotton balls black by placing the black powder paint and talcum powder in a paper bag. Shake the bag to mix the paint and talcum powder. Drop in the cotton balls a handful at a time and shake again to color them. Remove the cotton balls by the handful and shake off the excess powder.

       Math with Nursery Rhymes

How Many Bags Full?

Color in the number of bags you have filled with cotton.

Count the cotton balls.

Put an X on the bag with the most.

How Much Wool?

Center Activity and Bulletin Board

Use the sheep pattern on page 38 and flap pattern on page 39 to create a charming counting bulletin board.

Reproduce as many copies as you want numbers on your board. Write a numeral on each sheep's body. Glue that same number of cotton balls on the flap. Glue the flap to the sheep.

Cover a bulletin board with blue and green paper to create a meadow. Pin the "flock of sheep" down low on the board so children can reach them.

Children count the cotton balls on the sheep, say the number softly out loud, then lift the flap to see if they are correct.

Variation:

Make a set of sheep containing number words or simple computation problems.

Counting Books

Use the same patterns to create individual counting books. Give each child a sheep pattern and ten "flap" pieces. Students write a numeral and a set of dots on each flap piece. They put their sets in sequential order and staple them on the sheep pattern.

Note: Reproduce this sheep pattern to use with the activities on page 37.

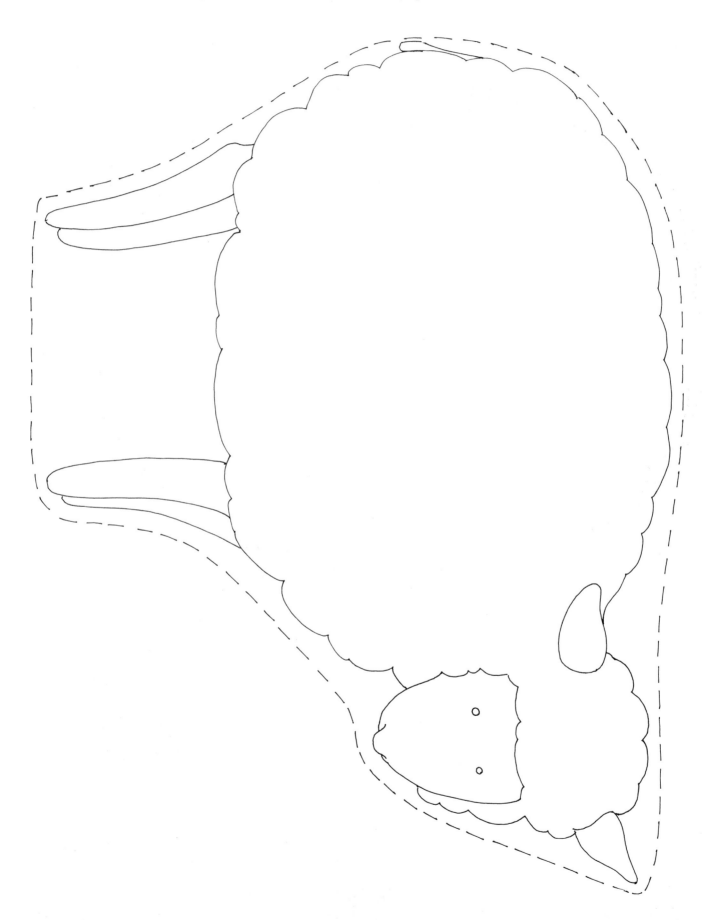

Math with Nursery Rhymes

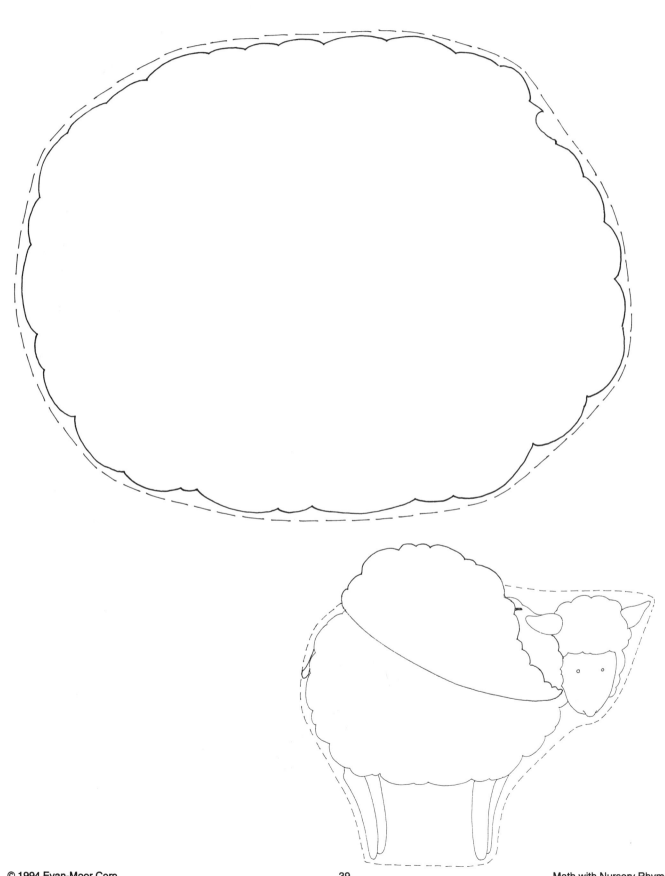

Math with Nursery Rhymes

Note: Students reinforce counting skills by making these bags.

1. Cut out the bag.
2. Fold on the lines.
3. Write the numerals.
4. Draw a set.

It's In the Bag
A Counting Activity

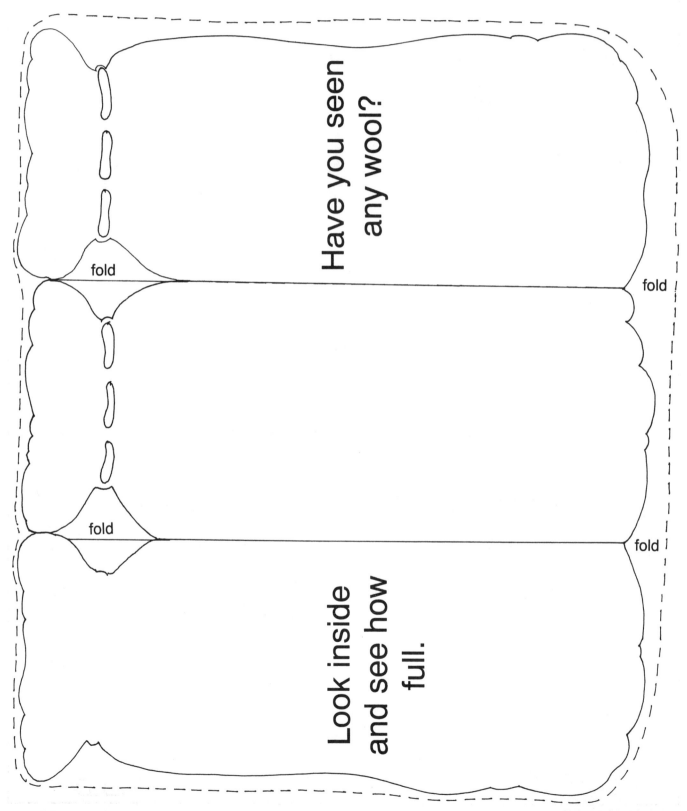

Have you seen any wool?

fold

fold

fold

fold

Look inside and see how full.

Math with Nursery Rhymes

Pease Porridge Hot

Pease porridge hot, pease porridge cold

Pease porridge in the pot nine days old.

Some like it hot, some like it cold

Some like it in the pot, nine days old!

 Math with Nursery Rhymes

Pease Porridge Fun

What Is Porridge?

Explain to students that porridge is a soft food made from cereal or meal boiled in water or milk. Let students suggest their favorite types of porridge. In this nursery rhyme we are talking about a porridge made from dried peas.

Bring in a favorite recipe for split pea soup and share a cooking and tasting experience with your children. Perhaps students would also enjoy making other types of porridge: instant oatmeal or cream of wheat.

Nine Days of Peas

Create a set of nine paper plates containing dried peas representing sets from 1-9. Glue the peas to the plates and write the correct number on the back of the plate to make the activity self-checking. Place the plates in a math center and let students count and sequence the plates.

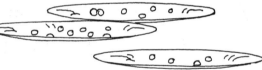

Dried Peas Center

Put out a set of nine bowls and a container of dried peas (whole ones work best here as they are easier to count). Put a set of cards (numerals, number words, simple addition/subtraction facts) in the center. The child selects a card and uses the bowls and peas to show the number or answer indicated by the card.

Nine Days Old

Make a batch of real "pease porridge" (thick split pea soup) for children to taste. Then review the rhyme and talk about how some like it nine days old. Put some in a dish, cover with plastic wrap and place it in a refrigerator. Mark off the calendar for the next nine days, then look at the porridge. Does it still look tasty? Has mold begun to grow? Could you really eat it after nine days?

Pease Porridge Hot
Action Verse

Pease porridge hot,
(Stir, and then wipe brow from heat.)

Pease porridge cold
(Hug body and shiver.)

Pease porridge in the pot,
(Pretend to stir a large pot.)

Nine days old.
(Hold up nine fingers.)

Some like it hot,
(Wipe brow from heat.)

Some like it cold,
(Hug body and shiver.)

Some like it in the pot,
(Pretend to stir a large pot.)

Nine days old!
(Hold up nine fingers, and then count one-two-three-four-five-six-seven-eight-nine!)

Math with Nursery Rhymes

Math Skills: counting; problem solving; simple addition and subtraction; ordinal numbers

Peas in a Pot

Take masking tape and make a large "pot" on the floor. Select nine children to be "peas." Give each child a large green pea cut from construction paper. Have them move in and out of the "pot" to dramatize math problems. Add other characters to your dramatization if you wish. The example below includes a cat and a cook.

"The cook put six peas in the pot."
(The cook taps six children to go into the pot shape.)
"He added three peas."
(Three more children are tapped and step into the pot.)
"How many peas were in the pot?"

"Along came his hungry cat. She gobbled up five of the peas. Bad cat!"
(Have the cat come by and tap five peas, who then leave the pot.)
"How many peas were left in the pot?"

"The cook came back and decided he needed more peas.
He put two more peas in the pot. How many were in the pot now?"

Continue the story for as long as you wish, having children give answers as you go along. Change "actors" frequently so everyone gets a turn.

Extension

Make a set of large construction paper peas containing numbers or number words. Pass them out to your children. Ask them to put the numbers in order. Once they have formed a line, have the "peas" respond to statements such as the following:

"The last pea sits down."
"The third pea turns around."
"The second pea in line goes to the drinking fountain."
etc.

The Old Woman in the Shoe

There was an old woman
who lived in a shoe.
She had so many children
she didn't know what to do.
She gave them some broth
with slices of bread,
And hugged them all soundly,
and sent them to bed.

Math with Nursery Rhymes

Shoe Business

A Shoeful of Happy Learners

Make a huge shoe from butcher paper. Make windows enough for each child in your classroom. Put a photograph or self - portrait in each of the windows.

Discuss the kinds of homes your children live in. Give each child a sheet of paper. Have them draw their own homes, putting themselves and other people living in their home in the windows. Display these around the bulletin board.

Shoelaces

Have everyone bring in a shoelace. Set them all out on the floor. Line them up from shortest to longest. Get out a yardstick and let the children measure their shoelaces. How many shoelaces tall are they? Have them go home and find out how many shoelaces tall their parents are.

Shoe Size

Materials:
• Childrens' shoes
• Shelf paper

Directions:
Children remove their right shoes. Working in groups of six, have them arrange the shoes shortest to longest. Lay the shoes on a sheet of shelf paper. Trace around the shoes.

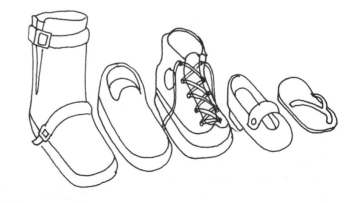

Note: Have children draw faces in any number of the windows they choose. Have them count and write down the number of the children who live in their shoe.

Who Lives in the Shoe?

_____children live in this shoe.

Math with Nursery Rhymes

Shoe Kids

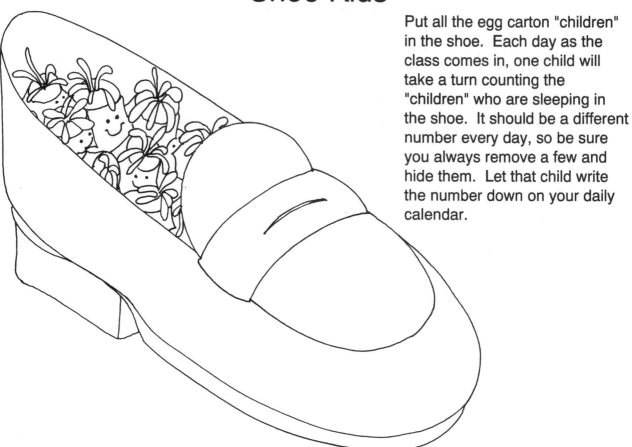

Put all the egg carton "children" in the shoe. Each day as the class comes in, one child will take a turn counting the "children" who are sleeping in the shoe. It should be a different number every day, so be sure you always remove a few and hide them. Let that child write the number down on your daily calendar.

Let each child make a special little "child" out of an egg carton section. Use these "children" for counting experiences.

Materials:
- sections from cardboard egg cartons
- colored yarn cut into 3-4 inch (7-10 cm) lengths
- glue
- colored markers
- your daily calendar
- a large slipper or loafer

Directions:
Have each student select yarn for his/her child's hair. Have students glue the hair to the top of the egg carton section. Now children can use the markers to make the faces.

Math with Nursery Rhymes